D1467498

RAIL 15 PORTFOLIOS

The 30s and 31s

Compiled by Peter J. Robinson

First published 1991

ISBN 0 7110 1967 3

© Ian Allan Ltd 1991

Published by

IAN ALLAN LTD

Terminal House Shepperton TW17 8AS
Telephone: Walton-on-Thames (0932) 228950
Fax: 0932 232366   Telex: 929806 IALLAN G
Registered Office: Terminal House Shepperton TW17 8AS
Phototypeset and Printed by Ian Allan Printing at their works at
Coombelands in Runnymede, England

Front cover:
No 31296 *Amlwch Freighter* was the first Class 31 to be named, but several other namings have since taken place. One of these was 'skinhead' No 31444, upon which the name *Keighley & Worth Valley Railway* has been bestowed. It is seen here on 26 May 1989 filling in for a Class 143 railbus as it romps along the Durham coast at Hart with the 14.59 Middlesbrough to Newcastle, formed of a BG and two Trans-Pennine TSOs. This locomotive coincidentally was 'all the fives' No D5555 when new to Ipswich in October 1959, and has now celebrated its 30th birthday in the Immingham Departmental pool. *P. J. Robinson*
Pentax 6 × 7 150mm   Fujichrome 400 1/1000, f6.1

Introduction

If longevity can be taken as a reflection of the success of a class of locomotives, the Brush Type 2s, later Classes 30 and 31, will certainly prove to have been one of the most successful British diesel designs. First introduced in 1957, 263 were eventually built, of which 190 were still running at the beginning of 1990.

Their durability owes much to their massive construction, weighing between 108 and 111 tons, compared with a Type 5 3,300hp 'Deltic' weighing 102 tons and contemporary Type 2 Classes 25 and 26 weighing 74 and 75 tons respectively. This weight necessitated three axled bogies, of which only the outer ones were powered.

For over 30 years the 31s have gone about their allotted tasks in an undemonstrative way, having aroused very little interest amongst the railway enthusiast fraternity. However, the disappearance of most of the other first-generation diesel designs has resulted in increased interest in the 31s, with congregations of enthusiasts forming at such locations as Dawlish and Aller Junction to record the summer Saturday holiday trains from Northwest England which have taken three pairs to Paignton in recent summers.

Having supplanted steam locomotives on some passenger duties when they were first introduced, the 31s were displaced in their turn by diesel multiple-units (DMUs). However, many have survived to turn the tables by replacing these same DMUs, by then life-expired, in the 1980s — in many cases both locomotives and coaches being older than the units they were succeeding. Train-heating boilers in the 31s have given way to electric train heating (ETH) and the 70 units fitted with ETH have been reclassified as Class 31/4.

Apart from the brief aberration in 1959 when D5578 and D5579 appeared in experimental colours, these machines have spent most of their lives painted in fairly drab liveries — the initial rather tasteful greens and grey having given way to 'corporate' blue in the mid-1960s. Latterly these 'ugly ducklings' have become a little more 'swanlike', by sporting the various grey Railfreight liveries. Sadly, this improvement is counterbalanced by the adoption of the ill-conceived slug grey in which the departmental locomotives will now be painted.

Despite the arrival of Class 60 freight locomotives and the East Coast main line electrification, 20 Class 31 overhauls are scheduled for 1990 and 1991 — which means that some of these gentle giants may well reach the ripe old age of 35 years.

With such a long life span, the choice of a representative selection of pictures has proved difficult, a problem complicated by the paucity of pictures pre-1975, presumably due to photographers' preoccupation with more glamorous power and the overreaction of many to the end of steam.

I am very grateful for the generous assistance of many fellow photographers and hope that this album does justice to a class of locomotives which will no doubt attract increasing interest as numbers dwindle. It seems likely that there will be retrospective recognition of the significant contribution made by the Brush Type 2s to the post-Beeching railway regeneration.

Peter J. Robinson
Tynemouth, 1990

Frontispiece:
On a duty for which Class 31s are most likely to be remembered, No 31466 coasts downhill through Buxworth cutting near Chinley, powering the 12.43 Cleethorpes to Manchester (Piccadilly) at 15.21 on 31 August 1984. *Robin Lumley*
Pentax 6 × 7 150mm Ektachrome EPD200 1/1000, f4.5

Left:
Restored to the condition in which it made its first public appearance at the head of the 10.36 Liverpool Street to Clacton on 13 November 1957, No D5500 poses for the camera at Grosmont, on the North Yorkshire Moors Railway, in May 1978. By this date it had been incorporated into the National Collection of preserved locomotives after withdrawal from service as No 31018 in July 1978.

The first 20 Class 31 locomotives were delivered during 1957-58, all to the ex-Great Eastern area in which they remained for their full 20-year lifespan. After restoration, No D5500 spent some time during 1978 working trains over the heavily-graded North Yorkshire Moors line between Grosmont and Whitby before retreating to the sanctuary of the National Railway Museum, having suffered serious tyre wear on the preserved line's sinuous curves.
J. R. P. Hunt
Pentax SPF 50mm Kodachrome 25 1/250, f3.5

Left:
Only days after outshopping from overhaul at Doncaster, No 31178 poses at Gateshead on 16 September 1987, resplendant in red-stripe Railfreight livery. In the author's opinion this livery is equally as flattering as the original green and grey combination in which, as No D5599, this machine was delivered new to Hornsey (34B) depot in March 1960. Now based on the LMR at Bescot in the Departmental Engineers pool (DCMA), it faces the indignity of having this attractive livery replaced by the slug-like all-over grey Departmental colour if it should survive another overhaul. *P. J. Robinson*
Pentax 6 × 7 105mm Takumar
Ektachrome·EPD200 1/125, f11

3

Left:
At 5.39pm on 10 May 1958, only a few months after delivery, No D5505 heads the 3.45pm Norwich to Liverpool Street past semaphore signals at Witham (now in the heart of 25kV electrification territory). The marker discs to indicate type of train are clearly visible — there were two others: one placed centrally above the coupling and the other 4ft above it, approximating to the four headlamp brackets on steam engines. Renumbered to 31005 this locomotive was withdrawn from Stratford in February 1980 and cut up at Doncaster works one month later. *R. C. Riley*
Agfa Silette ˙50mm Soligon Kodachrome (8ASA) 1/250, f2

Left:
No D5514 makes a fine sight on 28 February 1959 climbing Bethnal Green Bank on the 12.10 Liverpool Street to Cambridge, which comprised a mixture of ex-LNER Gresley and Thompson-designed coaches as well as some BR Mk 1 vehicles. The first batch of Class 31s were nicknamed 'toffee apples' because of the bulbous shape of their control handles. Under the 1972 TOPS-style renumbering this locomotive became No 31014 and eventually was converted to train heating unit No 968015, before being cut up at Doncaster in June 1983. *R. C. Riley*
Agfa Silette 50mm Soligon Kodachrome (8ASA)
1/250, f2

Left:
On a service in which it was to become involved again nearly 20 years later, No D5686 drifts downhill through Edale in March 1965 at the head of 2P52, a Manchester (Central) to Sheffield (Midland) local, formed of a BR van and three ex-LMS Stanier design coaches. About to be superseded by DMUs when this picture was taken, these trains reverted to Class 31 haulage in the mid-1980s when the units became life-expired. Having by then been renumbered 31258, this locomotive was fitted with electric train heating

equipment in February 1984 at Doncaster, becoming No 31434 as a result. It then re-entered traffic on the same South Trans-Pennine services that it is seen on here, replacing the same DMUs which had displaced it nearly 20 years ago. *B. J. Staniland*

Above:
One of the early members of the second batch of Class 31s constructed, No D5528 was delivered new

to Norwich (32A) in April 1959. It is seen here on 23 July 1966 showing Class H (now Class 8) headcode passing the typical Midland Railway signalbox at Bennerley Junction in the Erewash Valley, powering an Ashwell to Frodingham train of iron ore. The overbridge, still extant but disused today, carried the ex-Great Northern Grantham to Derby (Friargate) line. Now numbered 31110, this locomotive is currently based in the Sheffield area at Tinsley. *Bill Chapman*
Ektachrome X 64ASA

7

Left:
Once the early members of the class had seen wider service, concern was expressed at the number of fatalities among permanent way staff not hearing or seeing them coming. It was felt that the mainly green livery contributed to the problem as they tended to merge into their surroundings. In an attempt to improve visibility two locomotives were painted in brighter liveries: No D5578 was light blue and No D5579 in bronze gold (sic). Here is the latter, five years after delivery new to Stratford in January 1960, heading a typical mixed freight through Downham Market on 22 May 1965. Readers may take their own views about the colour but the fact that no further locomotives were so painted and the subsequent addition of the yellow panel suggest that the initiative was unsuccessful. No D5579 became No 31161 and then, in February 1988, was the final Class 31 to be fitted with electric train heating equipment, becoming No 31400. It is now based at Crewe in the General Parcels pool (RxxA). *J. E. Feild*
Kodak Retinette Agfa CT18 1/250, f4.5

Above:
No D5825, which was delivered to Sheffield Darnall (41A) in November 1961, was still working from that depot on 30 April 1966 when it was heading a typical mixed freight train of the period up the Midland main line past Duffield. The amount of steel traffic comprised in the load suggests that the train was from the Sheffield area, probably en route to Toton. Now No 31292, the locomotive is today allocated to Bescot. *Michael Mensing*
Nikkorex F 50mm Nikkor Agfacolor CT18 1/500, f3.5

Far left:
On a service long since withdrawn, No D5551 penetrates well into London Midland Region territory powering the 12.40 Harwich (Town) to Rugby (Midland) on 22 May 1965. It is approaching its final destination by taking the flyover junction past Clifton Mill to reach the south side of Rugby (Midland). No D5551 was delivered new to Ipswich in September 1959 and was no doubt working from there at the time of this picture. It is now numbered 31450 and is allocated to the Crewe Parcels fleet, in which its ETH facility is needed for working overnight postal traffic. *Michael Mensing*
Nikkorex F 50mm Nikkor Agfacolor CT18
1/500, f2.8

Left:
The same locomotive, No D5551, awaits departure from Ely with a King's Lynn to Liverpool Street train on 13 August 1966. Today it is one of the four Class 31/4 conversions with a 'skinhead' cab profile (ie no roof-mounted indicator panel), along with Nos 31418, 31444 and 31461. *Bill Chapman*
Ektachrome X64

Left:
The Anglo-Scottish border was infrequently breached by Sassenach Class 31s, principally due to lack of traction knowledge of this class amongst drivers north of the Border. Any which did venture into Scotland were invariably on workings which involved return to the sanctity of England in the hands of the same driver who drove north. In the circumstances No 31408 was quite a surprise on 21 April 1984 when it was seen approaching Longniddry powering a train of empty Mk III sleepers from Ferme Park to Aberdeen to form an overnight Stonehaven to King's Cross train for the Rudolf Steiner school that evening. No 31408 was new to Finsbury Park in September 1960 as No D5692 and is now in the Crewe-based Parcels pool (RxxA). *P. J. Robinson*
Pentax 6 × 7 105mm Ektachrome 200EPD 1/1000, f5.0

Above:
Looking very much at home in the broad acres of eastern England, in which they have been a feature of railway operations for so long, Nos 5574 and 5670, both in 'Corporate' blue with all-over yellow noses, jog along the East Coast main line between Newark and Grantham with a typically varied partially braked freight on 26 April 1973. Coincidentally both of these locomotives, now Nos 31156 and 31242, remain in eastern England at Immingham in the Petroleum (FPLI) and Departmental pools (DCEA) respectively. The former is still in Corporate blue — a livery it will have carried for nearly 20 years. *C. J. Ferris*

13

Left:
A view of the driver's position in No 31272, taken at Stratford on 26 April 1975. This would have been comfort indeed for the drivers at March Depot (31B) who, in 1961, exchanged their steam locomotives (including Classes B17, D16, B12 and J15) for this and other Class 31s. *J. E. Feild Canon FX 28mm Agfa CT18 1/30, f4*

Right:
Doncaster Plant has been responsible for heavy repairs and periodic overhauls of Class 31 for over 30 years. Two Class 31/4s, Nos 31404 and 31418, are seen here undergoing heavy repairs in the Crimpsall erecting shop. Whilst No 31404 (ex-No D5605) has roof-mounted indicator panels, No 31418 (one of the earlier deliveries as No D5522) has none; instead it has extra marker light openings, where the headcode discs were originally. *Les Nixon Pentax 6 × 7 105mm Super Takumar Ektachrome 200EPD*

Right:
No 5843, having lost its 'D' prefix and acquired full yellow ends, gravitated from Darnall, where it was first allocated in May 1962, to the Western Region. On 31 August 1972 it was caught by the camera fulfilling a duty with which the class was to become increasingly familiar — dragging failed DMUs, in this case along the sea wall at Teignmouth with a three-car Cross-Country unit. This locomotive became No 31310 in 1972, and then upon fitting with ETH in 1974 was renumbered 31422; it is now a Crewe-based Parcels Sector locomotive.
G. W. Morrison
Pentax K1000 50mm Kodachrome 25 1/500, f2.8

Far right:
On 29 June 1977, carrying out a duty which Class 31s have now performed for over 25 years, No 31316 ambles round the curves at Wylam on its return journey to Tyne Yard with the daily Hexham trip. The mini-Sydney Harbour bridge in the background used to carry the North Wylam loop, but is now merely a footbridge. New to Sheffield Darnall as No D5850 in June 1960, No 31316 was fitted with ETH at Doncaster in June 1984 when it was renumbered 31446 and is now based at Bescot in the DMCA Midland Region Departmental pool. *Mrs D. A. Robinson*
Pentax 6 × 7 105mm Super Takumar
High Speed Ektachrome 64 1/500, f4.5

Right:

In 1976 when British Rail quoted Cleveland Potash terms for handling the output from their massive new mine at Boulby, North Yorkshire, it was on the basis of haulage by pairs of Class 31s. In fact, because of their A1A bogies on which only two of the three axles are powered, they were not entirely suitable, frequently slipping to a stand on the climb away from the mine and again on the climb on to the top of Hunt Cliff near Brotton. This traffic necessitated the reinstatement of about three miles of the coastal Saltburn to Whitby line between Skinningrove and Boulby. A long embankment at Skinningrove was replaced by a new bridge which is seen here (lower) being negotiated in 1980 by Nos 31141 and 31278; they are proceeding towards Boulby with six of the large purpose-built bogie hoppers which ply between the mine and Teesport.

The upper picture shows Nos 31141 and 31130 breasting the summit at Hunt Cliff with a combination of empty diesel oil tanks and loaded potash hoppers on 5 October 1977.

Both: P. J. Robinson

Top: Pentax 6 × 7 105mm Ektachrome 64 1/500, f4

Bottom: Pentax 6 × 7 105mm Ektachrome EPD200 1/500, f5.6

Left:
No 31423 makes a surprise appearance when it arrives at Peterborough on Sunday 28 August 1977 at the head of the 17.10 King's Cross to Leeds. As this train was rostered for a Deltic, No 31423 was rather a diappointment, but it had certainly acquitted itself well, having lost only two minutes — despite having available well under half of the horse power of its larger stablemate. One of the second batch of convertees to Class 31/4, this machine is now part of the Crewe-based Parcels Sector pool (RxxA) and is the first class member to carry BR main line livery. *P. J. Robinson*
Pentax 6 × 7 105mm High Speed Ektachrome 64 1/500, f4

19

Left:
In April 1978 on one of the very rare occasions when a preserved diesel has run on BR lines under its own power, the restored No D5500 heads away from Teesside with its distinctive transporter bridge. The Class 31 is on the Whitby line towing 'Q7' 0-8-0 No 63460, en route for the North Yorkshire Moors Railway at Grosmont. No D5500 spent a season on the NYMR before returning to the sanctuary of the National Railway Museum, where it remains today. The Q7, also part of the National Collection of preserved locomotives, is still at Grosmont, where restoration to running order by volunteers of the North Eastern Preservation Group is almost complete. *John Hunt Pentax SPF 50mm Kodachrome 25 1/250, f2.4*

Above:
In ex-works 'Corporate' blue livery on 3 August 1977, No 31289, at that time a regular performer in the Northeast, chirps merrily away from Tyneside powering the featherweight evening Newcastle to Morpeth parcels, which, on this occasion, was double the normal load. *P. J. Robinson Pentax 6 × 7 105mm High Speed Ektachrome EH 1/1000, f3.5*

Right:
Another of the Gateshead trio of 31/4s, No 31406, sees the New Year in by working a Sunderland to Newcastle football special in connection with the local 'derby' on 1 January 1980. In the still frosty air the sound of the ex-works 31 working flat out to achieve about 70mph with its 11 packed coaches could be heard for about six or seven minutes. No 31406 was new to Stratford in June 1960 as No 5616, and is now in the Crewe Parcels fleet (RxxA). *Mrs D. A. Robinson*
Pentax 6 × 7 105 Super Takumar
Ektachrome 200EPD 1/1000, f4

Far right:
Class 31s have always been nocturnal animals due to their involvement in parcels, newspaper and mail traffic. No 31321 awaits departure from York on 12 November 1981 with a typical small hours duty, 4M38, the 01.47 York to Birmingham vans. Today, this locomotive, now No 31468, is based at Crewe in the Headquarters Divisional pool (DCQA).
David I. Rapson
Canon AEI 135mm Kodachrome 64 30sec f5.6

Far left:
For the whole of their lives, 31s have played a major role in the steadily reducing summer seasonal Saturday workings to coastal resorts; they can be seen even today on the Devon coast and at East Coast resorts on summer dated trains. On such a typical working No 31200 stands, on 22 August 1981, amid the splendour of Scarborough station, awaiting departure with the 11.10 (SO) to Sheffield. New to Ipswich (32B) in June 1960, 31200 is now one of the Crewe-maintained coal sub-sector fleet (FHHA) specifically dedicated to Sellafield Nuclear Flask traffic. *P. J. Robinson*
Pentax 6 × 7 105mm Ektachrome 200 EPD 1/125, f13

Left:
Another East Coast summer holiday working: on 19 September 1981, No 31245 descends Belstead Bank approaching Ipswich with a Saturday Liverpool Street to Lowestoft train, before taking the East Suffolk line. New to Finsbury Park (34G) as No D5673 in December 1960, this locomotive was withdrawn from Stratford in January 1987 and cut up there in March 1988. *P. J. Robinson*
Pentax 6 × 7 150mm Ektachrome 200EPD 1/500, f5.6

27

Left and Below:
The same locomotive, No 31166, in ex-works condition but 11 years apart. In Corporate blue on 9 August 1979 at Ouston Junction, Chester-le-Street awaiting a road on to the main line with a trainload of Consett steel and in freshly applied Departmental livery on 3 May 1990 shunting the Castle Cement terminal at Railway Street, Newcastle upon Tyne. In 1979 No 31166 was Thornaby-based but by 1990 was a member of the Bescot DCML pool. Readers may decide for themselves which of these two uninspiring liveries they prefer!
P. J. Robinson
Both Pentax 6 × 105m
1979 Ektachrome 200 1976 1/125 f13
1990 Fujichrome 400 1990 1/125 f19

Above:
On the occasion of another Northeast local 'derby' — this time between Sunderland and Middlesbrough on 14 November 1981 — No 31163, allocated to Old Oak Common, heads across the High Level Bridge at Gateshead with empty stock from Heaton Carriage sidings to form a 'footex' from Sunderland to Middlesbrough. Even the cheerful late autumn sunshine cannot disguise the disgraceful external condition of the locomotive, with its oil-ingrained sides and patches of flaking paint. However No 31163 is still soldiering on today, now based at Tinsley. *P. J. Robinson*
Pentax 6 × 7 150mm Ektachrome EPD 200
1/500, f6,3

Above:

The reduction in traditional local and short-haul freight duties has resulted in Class 31 assuming a higher profile in its third decade. One example was the use of a small pool of 7 Bristol-based 31/4s on South Wales/Bristol to Southampton/Portsmouth passenger services in the late 1970s/early 1980s. No 31401 skirts the River Itchen at an attractive location (Woolston) while powering the 14.10 Portsmouth to Cardiff on 29 May 1982. No 31401 was written off in an accident at Gloucester in February 1988. *John Chalcraft*
Mamiya 645 80mm Sekor Agfachrome R100s
1/500, f5.6

Above:

A rather unkempt No 31420 passes Tunnel Junction, Salisbury powering the 12.05 Cardiff to Portsmouth Harbour on 19 April 1980. This locomotive was first allocated, as No D5591, to Hornsey in February 1960, became No 31172 and then gained its present number when converted to 31/4 by the fitting of ETH equipment in 1974. It is now a member of the Midland Region Departmental pool at Bescot (DCMA). *Brian Denton Nikkormat 50mm Agfachrome 50 1/250, f4.5*

Above:

A motive power crisis on the North Yorkshire Moors Railway in the summer of 1982 necessitated an approach to BR for assistance. The Class 08 initially provided was too slow for the 18-mile line, but the hire of a Thornaby-based 31 proved ideal. Disc-fitted No 31134 gave invaluable assistance for several weeks and is here seen in the depths of Newtondale powering the 14.20 Pickering to Grosmont service on 17 August 1982. New to Ipswich (32B) in September 1959, No 31134 recently celebrated its 30th birthday back in its native Great Eastern territory at Stratford in the Aggregates pool (FALG). *Mrs D. A. Robinson Pentax 6 × 7 105mm Ektachrome 200 1/500, f5.6*

Right:

Enjoying a brief moment of glory on 3 December 1982, Nos 31403 and 31415 approach Annfield Plain with a Royal Train on the Consett branch in connection with a visit by His Royal Highness Prince Charles to the former steel town. As this line lost its passenger service on 23 May 1955 any passenger train was a rarity, but a Royal Train was almost unbelievable. Sadly the locomotives were prepared at Gateshead — a depot with no experience of locomotive cleaning — and were not really in the sparkling condition expected for a Royal Train, but they still made a brave sight in the wintry sunlight. *John Hunt Pentax SPF 50mm Kodachrome 25 1/250, f2.4*

Far left:
In 1983-4 Class 31 began to raise its profile as locomotive-hauled trains began to be introduced as successors to life-expired DMUs. Often the replacement Class 31 locomotives and Mk 1 steam-heated stock were older than the vehicles they supplanted. One such service was that from East Anglia to the Midlands. Here is 23-year old No 31246 accelerating away from Norwich (Thorpe) past the fuelling point with the 13.32 Norwich to Birmingham on 22 June 1984. New to Finsbury Park (34G) as No D5674, this locomotive was fitted with ETH equipment in November 1984 when it was renumbered 31455, and is now yet another member of the Crewe Parcels fleet (RxxA). *P. J. Robinson*
Pentax 6 × 7 150mm Ektachrome 200EPD
1/500, f8

Left:
Continuing their pursuit of the Trans-Pennine and InterCity DMUs, in 1984 Class 31s usurped these units on the Leeds-Morecambe services to which they had by then been cascaded. The replacement locomotives and stock were as old or older than the units they replaced and did not prove particularly reliable; they have now given way to Class 142 four-wheel railbuses. Here No 31440 heads the 13.36 Lancaster to Hull through attractive pastoral country near Clapham on 9 June 1984.
Paul Shannon
Olympus OM1 200mm Zuiko Kodachrome 64
1/250, f6.3

35

Left:
For the full 30 years of their lives 31s have been involved in deputising for failed or unavailable DMUs either by hauling replacement stock or towing the actual DMU. Here is one such occasion on 22 June 1984 with No 31226 towing a failed DMU over Reedham swing bridge, forming a Lowestoft to Norwich service. This locomotive is still allocated to the Anglia Region at Stratford where it is a member of the Aggregates pool (FALG). *P. J. Robinson*
Pentax 6 × 7 105mm Ektachrome 200EPD 1/500, f6.3

Right:
Another service upon which the later batch of 31/4 conversions replaced ageing DMUs was that from Humberside and Sheffield to Manchester and Liverpool via the Hope Valley. Here No 31455 shatters the still frosty air of a wintry South Pennine morning at Edale on 18 December 1984 with the 10.41 Manchester to Sheffield. *Les Nixon*
Pentax 6 × 7 105mm Ektachrome 1/500, f5.6

Right:
No 31305 conveys a fine sense of movement kicking up freshly fallen snow as it bursts out of Box Middle Hill Tunnel powering the Sunday Birmingham to Bristol Parcels on 10 February 1985. This beautiful picture is a just reward for the photographer's perseverance in reaching the location and no doubt waiting some time in the very cold conditions. No 31305 was new to Sheffield Darnall (41A) as No D5838 in April 1962 and is now based in Birmingham at Bescot in the Departmental fleet (DMCA). *John Chalcraft*
Mamiya 645 210mm Sekor Agfachrome 1005
1/500, f4.5

38

Above:
No 31117, which was delivered to Norwich (32A) in June 1959 as No D5535 prior to the introduction of the roof-mounted indicator panels, had, by 1985, migrated to Old Oak Common, where it became a minor celebrity. It was repainted there, receiving larger numerals which it still sported when it was transferred to Thornaby in late 1986. It ended its days there, being switched off for the last time in March 1987 and cut up at Doncaster in September 1988. It is seen here on 8 May 1985 at the attractive ex-GWR Yeovil (Pen Mill) station awaiting departure for Exeter with the Chipman's weed-killing train. *John Chalcraft*
Mamiya 645 210mm Zoom @ 180mm Sekor
Fujichrome 100 1/500, f5.6

Above:
Prior to the tragic loss of most of the newspaper distribution business to road transport, the country was served by a fascinating network of nocturnal van trains. In most cases the empty vans returned during the day and were frequently 31-hauled. The short-distance cross-Pennine Manchester to Leeds service was often formed by an attractively uniform rake of four-wheeled vans bearing Parcels Sector livery, and is seen here coasting downhill near Diggle on 12 April 1987 behind No 31166, now a Tinsley locomotive (FGWC). *D. H. Ballantyne Leica 50mm Kodachrome*

Right:
In 1983 Mr Ron Cotton was appointed Project Manager of the Settle & Carlisle route with a mandate to achieve a trouble-free rundown to closure. As he was a traditional career railwayman with a record of generating growth through promotional incentives, his proven abilities seemed inappropriate to his new position. Predictably, he saw the Settle & Carlisle as an asset rather than a liability and soon became engaged in discussion with the various local authorities. Aided by copious publicity, both specifically targeted and free in the news media, traffic levels began to increase with the result that the standard formation of the two daily trains of Class 31 and four coaches quickly grew to two Class 31s and 10 coaches. Nos 31448 and 31449 climb towards Ais Gill across Birkett Common under a louring Pennine sky powering the 16.35 Carlisle to Leeds on 31 August 1985.
P. J. Robinson
Pentax 6 × 7 150mm Ektachrome EPD200 1/500, f6.3

Above:

As part of the Provincial Sector Strategy for reinvigoration of the Settle & Carlisle route, a modestly revised timetable was introduced in May 1990 comprising more frequent lighter trains. Once again it was the turn of ageing Class 31s to take centre stage, inexplicably in view of the apparent availability of much more reliable Class 37/4s already owned by Provincial and displaced from Scottish services by Class 156 Sprinters. Predictably the '31s' have proved very unreliable with a very high failure rate — due to a combination of 'anno domini' and the very long time since most Class 31/4s last visited the works for a classified overhaul. Here No 31449 thrashes away from its Armathwaite stop heading the 17.58 Carlisle to Leeds on 19 May 1990 during the first week of the 'new' service.

P. J. Robinson

Pentax 6 × 7 150mm Fujichrome 400 1/500, f7.8

A small number of Class 31s have been fitted with miniature snowploughs, although the likelihood of being in the right place at the right time seems improbable. One example is No 31319, which, by 8 January 1987, had acquired grey Railfreight livery and integral headlights during a life-extending Heavy General Overhaul. It is seen here ambling through acres of de-industrialised land at Cargo Fleet, Middlesbrough, with Tees Yard trip P73 from the huge ICI Wilton Chemical complex to Tees Yard. One of the later deliveries, No 31319 was new to Stratford in August 1962 as No D5853 and is today based at Immingham in the Petroleum pool (FPLI). *P. J. Robinson*
Pentax 6 × 7 150mm Ektachrome EPD200
1/500, f5.8

This page:

Naming of locomotives became more common in the 1980s. On 3 September 1986, No 31296, by then 24 years old (new as No D5829 to Sheffield Darnall 1/62) found itself spruced up to be bestowed with the name *Amlwch Freighter* at the British Octel plant at Amlwch in Anglesey. This was the first Class 31 to be named and was a recognition of the value of the traffic derived from British Octel, for whose sole benefit the 15-mile branch from Gaerwen on the Holyhead-Bangor line to Amlwch remains open. This locomotive is unique in so far as it carries the Welsh translation *Tren Nwyddae Amlwch* on the other side. It is seen here (*left*) with both the duplicate nameplates presented to British Octel; leaving the plant after the naming ceremony with an LMS design saloon (*below*); and six weeks later (*right*) passing Pelaw on Tyneside with the varied load of 6R82, the 12.10 Speedlink service from Tyneside CFD to Ripple Lane, routed via Leamside. This name caused puzzlement on Tyneside — particularly the Welsh version! No 31296 is now a member of the Bescot Departmental pool (DMCA), where its duties seem unlikely ever to take it back to Anglesey.

L. Goddard 1&2
Nikon FG   Kodachrome 64   1/60, f12.3

P. J. Robinson 3
Pentax 6 × 7   150mm   Ektachrome 200EPD
1/500, f6.3

Above:

On 13 May 1989, Crewe Parcels Sector (RxxA) allocated No 31400 heads south along the Cumbrian Coast near St Bees past a fragrant carpet of bluebells. It is making its way to Manchester Longsight with the stock of the Huddersfield to Workington Postal, which will receive its weekly maintenance there. This locomotive bears a number which was not believed possible under the TOPs style system as it is effectively Class 31/4 No 0.

It is quite a distinguished machine, having started life in January 1960 as No D5579 in the experi-

mental bronze gold livery as shown on page 8. Renumbered to 31161 in the 1972 scheme it was withdrawn from service in early 1988 and was awaiting cutting up when No 31401 was written off in an accident at Gloucester. Very surprisingly, in view of the reduced requirement by then for ETH Class 31s, the decision was made to replace No 31401 — with the result that No 31161 was reprieved, overhauled and fitted with ETH at Doncaster and then renumbered 31400. There was no precedent for a No 0 as, when the general

renumbering to the present TOPS system was carried out, the individual first-of-class locomotives were allocated new numbers out of sequence, eg Nos D5500, D9000, D200, D6700 and D1500 became Nos 31018, 55022, 40122, 37119 and 47401 respectively. *P. J. Robinson*
Pentax 6 × 7 150mm Fujichrome 400 1/1000, f6

Left:
Only three of the London termini were regularly
served by Class 31: King's Cross and Liverpool
Street, virtually from the introduction of the class,
and Paddington from the 1970s. No 31461 is seen
here on 2 November 1985 in the heart of the urban
sprawl of West London heading through West-
bourne Park, bound for Paddington with the stock
to form an express to Penzance. Formerly
No 31129, this locomotive, as No D5547, was the
last of the early batch to be delivered without
roof-mounted indicators. However, there was a
reversion to the 'skinhead' profile on a few
locomotives between Nos 5552 and 5561, due to an
interruption to the supply of the indicator panels.
This machine is now based at Immingham in the
Departmental Headquarters pool (DWCQ).
John S. Whiteley
Pentax 50mm Kodachrome 64 1/500, f3.5

Above:

As wagonload freight continued to decline, lesser-powered units were assigned to an increasing extent to multiple operation of heavy block load trains. Class 31s were regularly diagrammed in pairs and here are Nos 31304 and 31201 powering the daily Preston docks to Lindsay oil refinery train of empty oil tanks. The train is seen entering Horbury Cutting bedecked in splendid autumnal colours on 28 October 1987. *John S. Whiteley*
Pentax 85mm Fujichrome 50 1/500, f3.5

Above:

Following the success at Finsbury Park of 'personalising' that depot's Deltic fleet by the application of white cab roofs and window surrounds, a modest attempt was made to relieve the drabness of the '31's' overall blue livery by the application of a white waistband to several of the Class 31/4s used principally for King's Cross empty coaching stock workings. One such example was No 31409, seen here on 10 April 1981 entering Sunderland station at the head of 3B01, the 17.21 Sunderland Brian Mills Depot to Peterborough parcels train. Having already reversed at Ryhope Grange Junction, this train will call at Newcastle before heading south up the East Coast main line. The dramatic statue is a War Memorial in Sunderland's Mowbray Park.
P. J. Robinson
Pentax 6 × 7 105mm Ektachrome 400 (EL)
1/500, f6.3

No 31229 has come to the aid of Nos 25904 and 25906 at the head of a Stanlow refinery to Leeds oil train passing Horbury Junction on 1 October 1986. Class 31s eventually completely ousted Class 25 from the Midland Region, taking over all their secondary freight, parcels and Departmental duties. No 31229 is now based at Thornaby, where it is one of the three members of the pool (FAMA) specifically dedicated to cement traffic from Eastgate, at the head of Weardale.
John S. Whiteley
Pentax 50mm Fujichrome 50 1/500, f3.5

Right:

Class 31s permeated North Wales when they supplanted Class 25s on secondary LMR duties during the 1980s. Immaculate Thornaby-based Departmental (DCEA) locomotive No 31285 bedecked in the attractive 'red stripe' Railfreight livery (a design pioneered unofficially on Class 37s at its home depot), passes the site of Mold Junction, near Chester, powering train 8F14 — the Penmaenmawr to Garston ballast working — on 16 February 1988. *David I. Rapson*

Canon AE1 50mm Kodachrome 64 1/500, f4.5

Above:
No 31414 leaves Frome past Clink Road Junction on 8 August 1988, towing failed three-car Cross-Country DMU set C885, forming the 08.35 Weymouth to Bristol. There are now no Class 31s based on the Western Region, thus such incursions are becoming increasingly rare. No 31414 is actually a Crewe-based Departmental locomotive (pool DCQA). *Brian Denton*
Nikkormat 50mm Kodachrome 25 1/250, f2.8

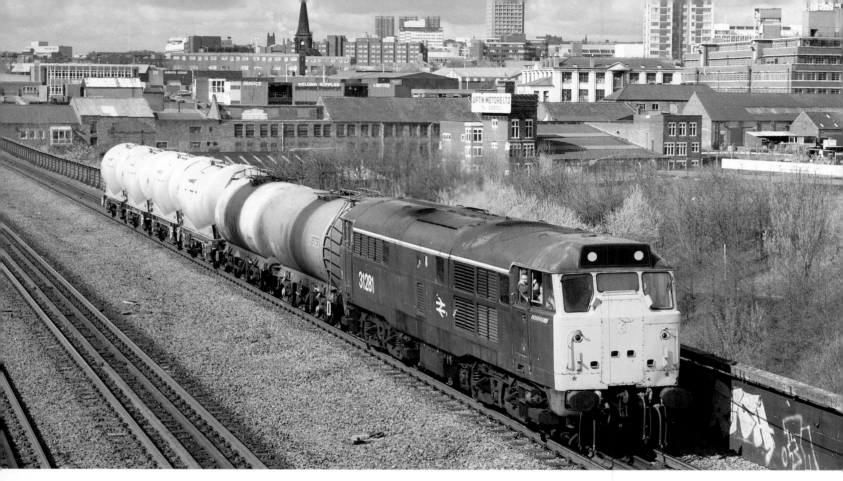

Above:

For several years the staff at Thornaby depot have sought ways to distinguish their locomotives. They pioneered the photographically-helpful red stripe around the bottom of the bodywork, which was later adopted officially. They also introduced the concept of depot symbols by adopting a white outline of a kingfisher on their locomotives, followed by a more colourful version. This was another initiative adopted nationwide with cast metal depot symbols now being fitted to all Freight Sector locomotives. Another initiative was the application of large numerals to several locomotives, including No 31281, seen here on 26 August 1988 crossing Byker Bridge, Newcastle heading for Heaton with a trip freight from Tyne Yard comprising two tanks of diesel fuel for the BR Traction Maintenance Depot and four cement tanks for the Blue Circle terminal. *P. J. Robinson* *Pentax 6 × 7 105mm Fujichrome 400 1/500, f8.5*

Above:

There is a small pool, designated FAMA, of three Thornaby-based locomotives, Nos 31184, 31215 and 31229, specifically dedicated to cement traffic from the Blue Circle Eastgate works. The remains of the Weardale branch from Bishop Auckland remain open for this traffic. On 22 May 1989 No 31215 was being assisted by No 31230 from the Bescot Departmental pool. No 31215 is unique in so far as it has an indicator panel at one end but, due to accident damage, the rear cab has been replaced by a 'skinhead' profile taken from a withdrawn sister locomotive. This train is the 18.50 Eastgate to Tyne Yard seen here passing Frosterley at 16.00, running three hours early, as is customary with this train.

P. J. Robinson

Pentax 6 × 7 150mm Fujichrome 400 1/500, f8.5

Above:
The advent of the unreliable Class 142 and 143 railbuses had resulted in considerable work for Class 31s deputising for failed units by hauling short rakes of Mk 1 coaches or by towing geriatric, first-generation DMUs. No 31465 is seen here against the peeling paintwork at Bolton at it makes its booked stop with the 13.32 Blackpool to Manchester provincial service. No 31465 is being hired to the Provincial Sector by its owners, the Departmental pool at Bescot. *Paul D. Shannon Olympus OMI 135mm Zuiko Kodachrome 64 1/250, f6.3*

Above:

A select group of eight locomotives now form pool FHHA, with the machines maintained at Crewe but operating from Workington on flask trains between nuclear power stations and Sellafield. All have been repainted into three-tone grey Railfreight livery bearing coal sub-sector decals of four black diamonds. On 10 May 1989, No 31270, fitted with half a snowplough, slips unobtrusively through the Tyneside conurbation as it approaches King Edward Bridge Junction, Gateshead with 7M60, the 09.25 (WO) Seaton-on-Tees to BNFL Sellafield nuclear flask train. Note the empty HEA coal hoppers serving as barrier vehicles and the obligatory brake van. *P. J. Robinson*

Pentax 6 × 7 150mm Fujichrome 400 1/500, f8.3

55

Above:

Closure of the West Coast main line for four weekends in March 1989 to facilitate essential engineering work resulted in diversion of through trains over the Settle & Carlisle line, the fate of which, at that time, was still in the balance. On the first two weekends the blockage was between Preston and Lancaster and, very enterprisingly, the planners decided to run trains between Carlisle and Lancaster in their booked paths. Everyone expected DMUs to be used but the London Midland Region further enhanced its standing in the eyes of enthusiasts by rostering this shuttle service for Class 31/4s. Here is No 31454, in filthy condition, surmounting the climb to Shap summit near Shap Wells with the 14.50 Lancaster to Carlisle on 11 March. With light loads the '31s' acquitted themselves very well. Timekeeping was exemplary with speeds as high as 96mph being recorded.

P. J. Robinson

Pentax 6 × 7 105mm Fujichrome 400 1/1000, f6.0

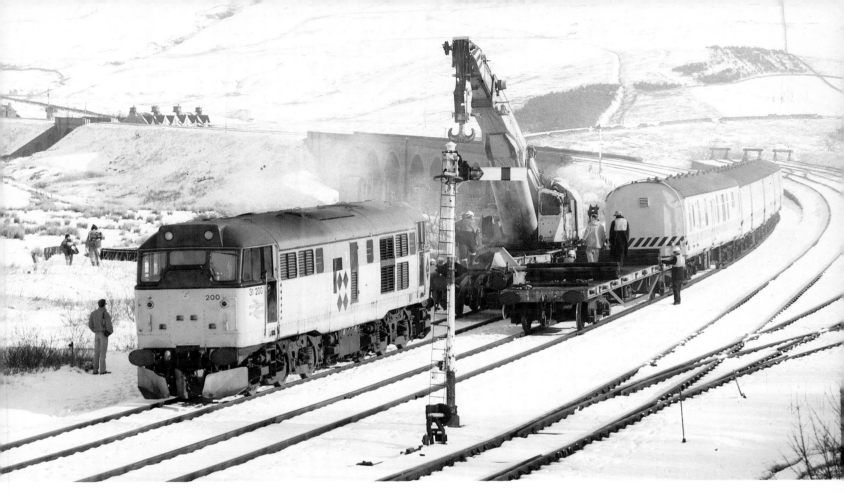

Above:
Locomotive No 31200, with a full set of snow-ploughs, officiates with the Carlisle Breakdown Train over the removal of the infamous Garsdale turntable on 26 February 1989. The turntable was lifted on to the bogie bolster wagon for delivery to the Keighley & Worth Valley Railway where it will be restored to working order. *P. J. Robinson*
Pentax 6 × 7 200mm Fujichrome 400 1/500, f8

Above:
Old habits die hard! Sixty-five years after the absorption of the Midland Railway into the LMSR there is still evidence of its 'small engine' philosophy which resulted in weekend summer holiday trains being worked from industrial cities to the coast by pairs of modestly-powered locomotives more at home on weekday freight workings. Nos 31467 and 31433 enjoy a breath of sea air at Horse Cove, Dawlish with the (very) late-running 10.10 (SO) Manchester to Paignton on 6 August 1988. The lateness of more than two hours was due to a signal failure at Bristol. *P. J. Robinson*
Pentax 6 × 7 105mm Fujichrome 400 1/1000, f6.3

Right:
As they grow older Class 31s continue to break new ground. One instance was a diagram including 1V66, the 17.10 (FO) Newcastle to Cardiff train, which appeared in the 1988 summer working timetable rostered for Class 31 haulage, although shown as an InterCity 125 in the public timetable. No 31437, in its 29th year, makes a brave sight on 10 June 1988, on full power, accelerating away from its Durham stop with six Mk 1 coaches — striving to avoid delay to following HST services. No 31437 is a member of the Bescot Departmental pool.
P. J. Robinson
Pentax 6 × 7 150mm Fujichrome 400 1/1000, f6.1

Left:
Well off the beaten track, Tinsley Speedlink (FGWC) No 31171 passes semaphore signals at Crosby mines on the freight-only Flixborough Quay to Scunthorpe branch with steel coil from Dragonby to Scunthorpe West Yard on 11 July 1989.
K. A. Davies
Pentax ME 50mm Ektachrome 100 1/250, f8

Bottom left:
Behind the foreground of Rosebay Willowherb the clean red stripe Railfreight livery of No 31271 combined with the ScotRail-liveried ex-LMS saloon makes for a colourful surprise heading north along the East Coast main line near Aycliffe on 27 July 1988. *P. J. Robinson*
Pentax 6 × 7 150mm Fujichrome 400 1/1000, f5.6

Right:
On InterCity duty — No 31402 is deputising for an electric locomotive on 7 May 1989, working the Sunday 08.40 from Manchester to Birmingham through Hednesford. This train had been diverted via Rugeley and Cannock Chase due to engineering work on the electrified Stafford to Wolverhampton route. *Hugh Ballantyne*
Leica Kodachrome 25 1/500, f2.8

Left:

As Class 31s have rarely, if ever, travelled north of the Forth-Clyde Valley there has been no chance of capturing them in the dramatic scenery of the various Highland lines. However, as a result of ousting Class 25 from its long-established LMR stamping ground in North Wales they now regularly penetrate Snowdonia by working the summer locomotive-hauled train between Llandudno and Blaenau Ffestiniog, utilising stock and locomotive off the holiday train from Stoke. No 31462 in the drab Departmental livery passes Roman Bridge on the 14.18 Blaenau Ffestiniog to Llandudno on 1 September 1989. Crewe-based (FHHA) Class 31s also work nuclear flask traffic beyond Blaenau to Trawsfynydd over the full length of this branch.
G. W. Morrison
Pentax K1000 50mm Kodachrome 25 1/500, f2.8

Above:

With the composition nicely balanced by the attractive semaphore signals at Wrawby Junction, Barnetby, Nos 31238 and 31305 in Railfreight — petroleum sub-sector — and red stripe Railfreight livery respectively, make a fine picture on 15 June 1989 as they head for Lindsey refinery with empty bogie oil tanks. With several members of Class 31 allocated to Railfreight pools we can expect to see more of the life-extended Class 31s repainted in this attractive three-tone grey livery. Although No 31238 is a member of the Immingham Petroleum pool, No 31305 is a Bescot Departmental locomotive. *J. S. Whiteley*
Pentax 90mm Kodachrome 64 1/500, f4

Above:
Chronic DMU availability problems at Newton Heath Depot, Manchester led to the welcome substitution on 2 September 1989 of locomotive and hauled stock on the monthly weekend 'Dalesrail' ramblers' special from that city to Carlisle routed via Preston, Blackburn and the Settle & Carlisle route, upon which it calls at all stations. Local enthusiasts were greatly encouraged by this change and even went to the length of preparing a very professional headboard to grace the front of the locomotive, which was expected to be a Class 47. Instead filthy, graffiti-covered 28-year-old No 31412 was provided; aesthetically, this machine suffers the handicap of carrying the abysmally dull Departmental all-over grey livery, made to look even worse in the sun-dappled beauty of Garsdale by the inclusion of an ex-works InterCity-liveried Mk 1 TSO as the first vehicle. As No D5692 this locomotive was new to Sheffield Darnall in March 1961. *P. J. Robinson Pentax 6 × 7 150mm Fujichrome 400 1/1000, f6.3*

Rear cover:
Following the demise of No 97201 (a former Class 24 used by the Derby Research Division), No 31298 was transferred to Derby, renumbered 97203 and repainted in the attractive Research Division livery. Unfortunately it was condemned in July 1986 as a result of fire damage and No 31326, the penultimate member of the class, was drafted in to take its place, becoming No 97204 and assuming Research Division livery. It is seen here passing through Crewe station on 5 August 1988 towing Park Royal DMU cars Nos 97508/90 forming train IT20, the 06.30 Derby to Workington Test.
David I. Rapson Canon AEI 50mm Kodachrome 64 1/500, f4.5